WHAT YOUR PARENT IS TRYING TO SAY

Chinaemerem Daniel

To my mom, Anthonia Daniel, for being the best parent in the world.

Contents

Introduction

Are you also the one who feels that their parents don't understand them? All your reasons and logic always seem to fall on deaf ears, as if they are not listening or both of you are speaking different languages. You invariably argued about everything under the 'roof:' curfews, makeup, dress code, sleepovers, debated over friends, or fought the never-ending battle over screen time.

Does it ever cross your mind why your parents behave the way they do? Asking so many questions about your day, saying no to harmless things, or making you feel like you're not good enough. Yes, but guess what? Maybe they're thinking the same thing: why can't my child see I'm just trying to help?

Fret no more because this book is here to help you translate their language to you.

This book is based on the simple fact: parents and kids love each other. However, and that's big however, sometimes, they are on different ends of the communication spectrum, seemingly speaking languages alien to each other. Call it generation gap, being overprotective, or being too ambitious, this communication gap often leads to miscommunication and frustration. And the gulf widens. A conversation with a parent trying to guide or protect can easily be assumed as criticism by the receiver. Conversely, when it's the child's turn to ask for independence, freedom, or understanding, the other side may perceive it as rebellion or disrespect.

I am sure the majority of you can relate to what I have written. How do I know that? Because we all have experienced that. You are not alone. Hence, the reason to write this book.

What Your Parent Is Trying to Say aims to bridge the widening communication gulf so that both parties can understand what is being said to them without any preconceived notions. Remember, the idea is to get parents and children on talking terms where they both are speaking the same language and understanding the non-verbal part as well. This is to help in building trust, empathy, and kindess as they try to figure out the words and actions of each other.

Before we start, let's just accept the fact that since we all are humans, we all are prone to mistakes. None is infallible. However, parents, despite their drawbacks or weaknesses, continue to give their best for their kids, and this is something that the younger generation needs to understand. Give your parents (and your kids) the benefit of doubt if and when they falter and try to move on from there. Only with this mentality will you be able to comprehend why they have a different perspective and how to get your words across to them.

CHAPTER 1:
Parents Are Humans

If you were walking down the street and somebody cut you off, and you looked over to see it was your beloved best friend. Our best friend can, at times, be a jerk, but at that moment, you wouldn't think, 'Oh, what a jerk.' You'd think, 'Oh, my gosh, what's going on? What has happened in their life to make them run this way? There must be some sort of an emergency.' Their internal life and reasons matter to you. When we see a person as a person, we see their internal motivations and the reasons for their behavior. When we see somebody as an object, we just see what they've done that bothers us. All we see is how their behavior is interfering with the stuff we're trying to do. We don't give any thought to why they're doing it or what rationale and understandable reasons they might have. Powerful stuff, right?

We often hold parents to near-impossible standards, expecting them to have all the answers, to be strong all the time, and to never make mistakes. Ever paused to think about your parents as individuals—not just as 'Mom' or 'Dad?' Beyond the roles they play in your life, they are human beings who had a life before you came along. They've faced joys and struggles, made mistakes, and carried dreams they might never have shared with you. What you sometimes dont realize is that your parents are figuring it out as they go, and, just like you, they're doing the best they can with what they know.

Every single day of their life is a learning curve. "In this very moment, they've never been the parent they are right now—not once in their life. They've never experienced the world as the parent of a 14-year, 6-month, 3-week, 2-day, 3-hour, 30-minute, and 50-second-old boy. It's an uncharted territory, every second, every breath. So, yes, they need a break—whew! That's a lot to handle!"

They Had a Life Before You

Long before they were your parents, they were kids just like you. They laughed with friends, broke the rules (yes, your parents were probably grounded at least once), and made embarrassing mistakes. They experienced heartbreaks, wrestled with insecurities, and navigated the ups and downs of growing up. Your parents have stories— ones you might not know yet. Maybe your mom dreamed of being an artist but chose a different path because life got in the way. Maybe your dad secretly loves music and still wishes he'd joined that band in high school. Those unspoken dreams and experiences shape who they are today, influencing the way they parent and connect with you. When you think about their lives before you, it's easier to see their struggles and decisions in a new light. They didn't become perfect, all-knowing adults the moment you were born.

Parents are the encompassing composition of every experience, mistake, triumph, and lesson they've encountered up until this very moment. They carry the weight of past decisions, the echo of their own parents' voices, and the hope of doing right by their children. Of course, we're just kids figuring things out ourselves, and we shouldn't have to deal with all this stuff. Yes! But when you pause and see them not just as parents but as people—with fears, flaws, and an endless desire to get it right—it gets a little easier to offer them grace. It becomes simpler to forgive the stumbles, to soften the misunderstandings, and to appreciate that they're learning too, step by step, day by day.

They Struggle Too

Society tends to create an unrealistic image of what it is to be a good parent. There's pressure to always be patient, to always be supportive, and never to mess up. Your parents feel this pressure as well, even if they never voice it. They struggle, too, and sometimes you can see it. Ever seen your parents having a bad day? Perhaps they've walked in the door from work depleted, short-fused over a minor thing, or appeared absent-minded and far-off. Those moments show us the truth about their humanity. They're not superheroes, and most of the time, they're not attempting to be villains. They're merely people living life with responsibilities while attempting to do good for you. You can't always see it because, as a younger person, the stresses they're under are not visible to you. They may be concerned about bills, stress at work, or internal insecurities. When they do things wrong or behave in frustration, it's usually because they're at their wit's end—not because they don't care.

Knowing their battles does not justify every cruel word or unjust decision, but it might allow you to view them more compassionately. They are not attempting to harm you; they are attempting to get through the struggles of life as parents, which is no easy task. This unrealistic expectation can cause them to feel guilty when they fail. Perhaps they screamed when they shouldn't have or were late to an important event in your life because they were too preoccupied. These instances don't define them, but they may be heavy on their conscience. They're doing their best, even when it doesn't necessarily seem that way to you.

Opening the Door to Understanding

When you begin to see your parents as people, not 'Mom' and 'Dad,' it has the potential to alter the way you connect with them. You may become more interested in who they are outside of being your parent. What was their childhood like? What things influenced them to become who they are now?

Asking these kinds of questions can lead to conversations that extend beyond rules and responsibilities. It's an opportunity to connect with them on a deeper level and see the world from their perspective. You may learn surprising things about their values and lives—and gain a new understanding of why they parent the way they do. Some arbitrary rule you've detested all your life could suddenly be understandable when you find out it's based on something that happened to them as a teenager, or you may discover sharing building dreams and aspirations you didn't even know you had.

Empathy - Interpret Their Intentions

Granting your parents' humanity doesn't equate to agreeing with all of their decisions, it does mean entering into those decisions with an open mind. Rather than assuming the worst about why they're saying no or implementing a rule, attempt to discern their intentions. More often than not, their decisions are motivated by love and a need to protect or provide for you, even if they don't always express it so well.

If you step back and consider the question, 'Why are they doing this,' you may realize that their behavior has a reason—even if they're annoying. Viewing your parents as humans with imperfections makes you bring more compassion to your relationship. You begin to see that their love isn't about being perfect or right—it's about attempting, showing up, and doing their best. And if you come to them in empathy, you open doors for more effective communication and understanding.

Rather than feeling as though you're on opposite sides, you begin to realize that you're on the same team, tackling life's obstacles together.

The Bigger Picture

Your parents' humanity does not make them more or less deserving of your love and respect. If anything, it makes their struggles more worthwhile and relatable. They're stumbling through the detours of life raising you, frequently without a definite road map or assurance that they're succeeding. So the next time you're frustrated or misunderstood, take a minute to recall: your parents are human beings first, parents second. They're not flawless, and they're not supposed to be. But they're trying their best for you, and that's something to acknowledge.

CHAPTER 2:
First-Time Parents Forever

Regardless of how assured or competent your parents might appear, they have never raised you before. Each child comes with their own set of challenges, pleasures, and surprises. Yes, even if they've already parented a child, you're a whole new learning curve. Parenting is not something that comes with an instruction manual, and every 'first' you experience in life, they're experiencing it right along with you—usually as first-time parents.

Parenting Without a Playbook

Consider this: your parents didn't receive a 'How To' manual upon your birth called 'Raising Your Child: The Perfect Way.' They were instead forced into a world of trial and error. Your first steps, first words, first tantrum—these were as new to them as they were to you, even more so if you have other siblings since they have to constantly monitor everything and everyone. And the learning doesn't end there. First day of school, first major test, first heartbreak, first job—every phase of your life brings new challenges for them. Just as you're learning how to navigate the world, they're learning how to guide and support you through it.

Envision being given a huge, complex puzzle but no image to work from. That's what parenting is like for most. Each decision—whether it's bedtime policy, screen time, or even which career guidance to provide—is dropping a piece of the puzzle without a clue whether it will fit. They are doing their best with what they know and what they have, and although their decisions may not always be perfect, they are nearly always made with your best interests in mind.

Parenting Is an Emotional Weight

It's simple to be caught up in what your parents are doing—the rules they establish, the decisions they make, the counsel they give—but behind all of that is an emotional process. Beyond the mechanics, parenting is also about connection, love, and development. When you get it right, they feel happiness and pride. When you fall, they feel your hurt intensely, beating themselves up for not being able to prevent it from happening. They struggle with guilt and self-doubt, wondering if they have let you down in some fashion. Parenting is an emotional roller coaster, and each turn and twist is driven by their love for you.

This emotional burden doesn't lessen with age. In fact, it may even become heavier. When you're a kid, they worry about your safety. As you age, their concerns shift to your happiness, well-being, and the future. Each phase of your life presents new joys and fears for them, and they hold these feelings even when they don't express them.

Parent's Evolve

It's important to recognize that your parents aren't static. The parents they were when you were a toddler are not the same parents they are today. They've grown, learned, and evolved—just like you have. They've adjusted their approaches, learned from their mistakes, and, in many cases, softened or hardened with time. Those who once panicked over every scraped knee might now be encouraging you to take risks. Earlier, they seemed overly strict about curfews; now, they trust you to manage your own time.

These changes reflect their growth as people and their willingness to adapt to your needs as you change and mature. But this growth isn't linear. Just like you, they'll stumble, make mistakes, and sometimes revert to old habits. This doesn't mean they're not trying; it simply means they're human. Sometimes, these changes come because you choose to step out of your corner and meet them in the middle, which can be unnerving.

They Sometimes Get It Wrong

All through history, we've seen a lot of famous stars become legends, and many times, it was because their parents pushed them really hard. Those parents were willing to do whatever it took, even if it meant being really strict at home. Back then, the kids probably didn't think it was fair or understand why their parents were so tough. Eventually, it was revealed that all that pushing and discipline were motivated by love and a desire to have the best for the kids, the future stars. Sometimes, what appears difficult to handle turns out to help us become something incredible in the future. Parents are not perfect and their choices won't always be what you want or think is best. Perhaps they say no to a party because they worry about your well-being or insist on a career choice because they believe it will ensure your success. These decisions, as painful as they might be, are a product of love and care.

Parents aren't perfect, and sometimes, you really do know more than they do. But just as they know things you don't, you have to learn how to tell them what you think without causing a fight. More often than not, even when you disagree with them, you can learn something from what they say. It's about being open-minded, listening, and somehow finding a way to discuss it. Sometimes, their choices are driven by their own fears or experiences. They may be attempting to safeguard you from blunders they themselves made or opportunities they didn't seize. At other times, they may just not have your perspective or information. After all, the world you're growing up in is not the same one they grew up in. It's okay to recognize that your parents are doing their best, but it does not require you to agree with everything. It can, however, help you come at disagreements with empathy, not resentment.

Meeting Parents Halfway

Living with your parents isn't always easy, especially since they're figuring things out for the first time, too. You have to find a way to make it work. Start by *practicing patience*. When a decision feels unfair, try to step back and see things from their point of view. They usually have reasons, which are often good, even if they don't explain them well.

Next, *communicate openly*. If you disagree with their rules, talk to them about it calmly instead of arguing. They might not change their minds, but they'll respect your honesty. Also, *remember that they're on a learning curve*. They're learning how to be parents, just like you're learning how to grow up. Offer alternatives so that they can get what they want while you get yours.

Finally, *show a little gratitude*. Even a simple "thank you" for what they do can mean a lot and help build a better relationship. It's all about meeting each other halfway.

The Bigger Picture

Even though it's tempting to dwell on their mistakes or choices you disagree with, they're always motivated by love. When you view your parents as fellow learners—individuals who are learning life and parenting along the way—you may find it less challenging to discuss things with them in a way that offers empathy and understanding. They aren't perfect, and they never will be. But they're trying, and that effort speaks volumes. Sometimes, you won't get everything you want from your parents—and that's okay.

Here's something to consider: learning *to stroke your parents' ego* a bit can actually help you get more of what you need. This doesn't require being insincere or excessively flattering. It's about *honestly* appreciating the things they do for you and letting them know you notice their efforts. When you sincerely inform them that you appreciate their advice and concern or express gratitude for something they have done, it makes them feel good about being a parent and more receptive to listening to you. Establishing this sort of positive rapport can simplify things at home. The secret is to establish the right balance: offer genuine compliments and then *back off*. Make them feel like they're making the last choice or that their own opinions count. When your parents feel respected and valued, they'll be more open to hearing your side of the situation without feeling defensive.

Obviously, you have to be sincere. Your parents will be able to tell whether you're just being nice for the sake of it, which will backfire instantly. So, only say what you really mean and don't overdo it. Disclaimer alert: this isn't about manipulating them or always getting your way; it's about making the relationship better and, more importantly, demonstrating that you're maturing too. Ultimately, a small amount of kindness, integrity, and understanding, when to let your parents have the way, will really advance you more than you realize.

So, next time you feel misunderstood or frustrated, take a moment to put yourself in their shoes. They're not only your parents; they are human beings dealing with the lifelong struggle of being first-time parents.

CHAPTER 3:
The Many Hats Parents Wear

Have you ever paused to think about all the roles your parents play in your life? They're not just 'Mom' or 'Dad.' They're providers, protectors, cheerleaders, teachers, decision-makers, and sometimes, even the villains of your story. All these roles come with unique responsibilities, emotional challenges, and constant juggling. Even more astonishing is the fact that the majority of the time, they are playing multiple roles simultaneously—multitasking supreme.

The Provider

As providers, your parents provide you with the necessities: food, clothes, shelter, education, and myriad other possibilities. This comes with sacrifices that you may not realize. They may be working excessively long hours, delaying trips or setting their own ambitions aside just to ensure you are provided for. The sacrifices are not always palpable or sensational. It might mean forgoing a night out with friends to put money away for your school trip or working late to assist you in completing a project, even after a long day of work. Their work in this role is motivated by love and a desire to provide you with a better life than they might have been able to provide for themselves.

Being a provider is not always about paying bills or eating dinner—it can be about making many sacrifices that aren't so apparent, especially to children. If your mom or dad can't attend your football game, it's not that they do not care; there may be other reasons that they are not willing to share with you so that you do not feel burdened or guilty, like working late to pay for your equipment, your school field trip, or even the home you live in.

There will be times when just one of your parents will be able to attend your functions while the other remains trapped in the office. It feels disappointing, but recognizing the 'why' will help greatly. The next time you get angry because your parents cannot come to something that matters to you or do not feel up to spending time with you, attempt to think about the grand scheme of things. They're doing it all for you even when it doesn't feel like they are. Realizing this can help you better understand them and perhaps even discover ways to demonstrate it to them.

The Protector

Your parents' instincts to keep you safe run deep. This role involves setting boundaries and making decisions that might not make sense to you—initially. Sometimes, they may overprotect, underestimating your ability to handle situations on your own. However, it doesn't mean they don't trust you; it simply means their protective instincts are incredibly strong. The challenge with this hat is 'balance.'

Here are ways that show what they are trying to do: take a curfew that feels unnecessarily early or a flat-out 'no' to something you're certain is harmless. It might feel like they're just trying to control your life, but in reality, it's their way of making sure you're safe, especially if they know the kind of dangers that can come out at night. A parent who works in a job where they see crime or accidents has a hard time with things like this. To be fair, we see these things happen all the time all around us. After seeing so much, it makes sense that they'd want to do everything they can to keep you out of harm's way. Think about why they care so much about who you hang out with and the places you go. It's not that they don't trust you. On the contrary, they know how easily the wrong atmosphere or the influence of the wrong people can lead to bad situations. They've seen this happen before, either in their own lives or to people they know, and they just want to make sure you don't end up in those same places.

Parents also worry about the things you can't see coming. Call it their gut feeling, sixth sense, or whatever; their experience has enhanced their analyzing powers over time, and often, they put it to good use. They know your strengths, but they also worry that you might not always be ready for what life throws at you. When they ask a million questions about your day or want to know every detail about where you're going, it's because they're trying to fill in the blanks—to make sure they're not missing anything that could hurt you. Even those moments when they seem overprotective, like insisting you text when you get somewhere or double-checking your plans, come from a place of love. They're not trying to make you feel small or like you can't handle yourself. They're just trying to make sure you have a safety net until you're strong enough to handle the world on your own. Basically, they are in a catch-22 situation. How much exposure is to be allowed and where to draw the boundary?

So, the next time you feel like they're being too much, try to remember that, in their eyes, protecting you is their most important job, even if it means being perceived a bit over the top sometimes. From your perspective, these decisions can seem overbearing or unfair. But from theirs, it's about protecting you from risks they've learned to recognize through their own experiences. Whether it's teaching you to look both ways before crossing the street or limiting your time online, their actions are guided by a desire to shield you from harm.

The Cheerleader

Recall how your parents have rooted for you, even when you doubted yourself. Whether it's clapping at your school play, celebrating your latest achievement, or simply telling you, "I believe in you," their role as your cheerleader is one of the most heartwarming hats they wear. Cheering for someone else requires emotional energy, especially when the person cheering is going through their own challenges. Even when life is tough for them, they often put on a brave face to show up for you and be your biggest supporter.

Cheering you can take different forms, too, and is easily missed because they don't always show it in obvious ways. Some parents might not say "I'm proud of you" or "You did amazing" as much as we'd like, but that doesn't mean they aren't supporting you; they are just doing it differently and you have to feel it. For example, when your parents say something like, *"I know you're not a B student."* Do not take it at face value; look deeper and you realize that it's their way of saying, *"I believe in your potential. I know you can do better because I've seen how smart and capable you are."* It's not about putting you down for getting a B—it's about reminding you of what you're capable of achieving. Sometimes, that's how they show they care and that they're rooting for you to succeed.

There are also the quieter signs of their support, like staying up late to help you study, driving you to every practice or rehearsal without complaining, or remembering to ask how your test went, even if they don't make a big deal about it. To be very honest, even if they do, that's okay sometimes. They are, after all, humans! They might not always express their pride in words, but it's there in the way they show up for you every day, in the sacrifices they make, and in the way they push you to be your best. You need to try to see it and pay attention to these small signs. It can help you see that even if your parents aren't super expressive, they're still your biggest fan. Recognizing this not only helps you appreciate them more but also makes it easier to understand that their tough words come from a place of love and high expectations—not disappointment.

To be fair, non-expressive parents need to do better, but having that extra grace to give them is something you can bring to the table. So, even when their support doesn't come with a big speech or a lot of praise, remember that they're still cheering for you every single day.

The Teacher

Parents are also your first teachers. My mom always pushed me to defy the concepts of textbook maths. She would say, "Sometimes it doesn't matter the approach as long as the rules are right." If you are asked to find the sum of all even numbers from 2 to 20, how will you go about it? While some of us may start by adding them one by one: $2 + 4 = 6$, then $6 + 6 = 12$, and so on. I prefer to pair them up, $(2 + 20)$, $(4 + 18)$, $(6 + 16)$..., realizing that each pair added to 22, and there were 5 pairs, making the sum 110 instantly! My mother emphasized that there's no single right way, or no hard and fast rule, to solve a problem. Different minds see different paths, but as long as the logic is right, they all lead to the same truth.

From tying your shoelaces to understanding the importance of honesty, your parents play a huge role in shaping the person you're becoming.

Sometimes, their lessons are subtle, like teaching the value of hard work through their actions. Other times, they're direct, like explaining why lying is wrong or why kindness matters. Teaching isn't always easy, though. I try to think about what thinking about my younger self must be like, urrrgh frustrating! Especially when I get in these moods, thankful that I had patient teachers. It requires patience, especially when lessons are met with resistance or frustration. But every lesson, no matter how small, is an effort to prepare you for life beyond their guidance.

The Villain Hat

Let's face it: there are moments when it feels like your parents are out to ruin your life. Yes, there are scenarios we've seen in movies and heard in stories where parents actually do this. That's why I wrote the book *When Your Parents Is Wrong*. In your story and in this scenario, the way I see it, your parent is indeed right. You want to do something to get far away from them. Slam the door because maybe they've grounded you, taken away your phone, or said "no" to something you really wanted. In these moments, it's easy to see them as the bad guy, the person standing in the way of your happiness. But even when they wear the 'villain' hat, it's rarely because they enjoy saying no. More often than not, their decisions are made out of love, even if it doesn't feel that way at the time. They're trying to guide you, protect you, or teach you something they believe is important. It is a hard thing to do, and truthfully, your parents aren't supposed to be your besties. Not all the time.

So throw them a curve ball; be mindful of your behavior in these moments. It is not the time to text them that long derogatory message or email or do something you will regret just to get back at them. This feeling will pass, and sometimes, the things we do in these moments can make a lasting impression. Pause, take out some time to reflect on the issue, and try to see how you can meet them in the middle, like I have been saying since the beginning of this book. When you give them grace and step into their shoes, you'll realize there are better ways to go about things. Plus, to be honest, they're mostly always right!

The Invisible Transitions Between Hats

Your parents don't wear just one hat at a time and don't have the luxury of sticking to a single role for long. One moment, they're enforcing a rule; the next, they're cheering you on. I don't know what kind of parent I am going to be because I would want my kids to sometimes violate my orders just to see how that feels, just kidding!

Parents might have to switch from being strict disciplinarians to comforting nurturers in the span of a single conversation without trying to be fake or manipulative. These constant transitions can be exhausting and emotionally draining, but that's what they have to do to ensure that they're doing their 'job' the right way and making sure you turn out great.

Imagine having to balance being a boss, a friend, and a teacher all at once. That's what your parents do every day, often without recognition. If you haven't noticed yet, after reading this book, you will start to notice these differences and switches. When you start to see these hats your parents wear, you will begin to understand how much they carry. They're not perfect—they're human. They get tired, overwhelmed, and sometimes make mistakes. But they're doing their best to fulfill these roles, often without a guidebook or a break.

How You Can Respond

Being appreciative of the complexity of your parents' role does not mean you have to say yes to everything they do or say. It doesn't mean you cannot become frustrated at times. It, however, does mean you can try to deal with your relationship more with empathy and patience.

- Acknowledge Their Efforts: A simple "thank you" can go a long way in letting them know that you notice and value what they do.

- Be Patient: If you don't agree with their choices, make an effort to realize where they are coming from before reacting.

- Talk to Them: If you feel frustrated or misunderstood, speak to them. Explain how you feel and why.

Your parents are not so much one thing; they're everything simultaneously. They're struggling to give you everything, keeping you safe, teaching you, and propping you up while getting through their own lives and issues. It helps to consider the burden of these things in order to observe them differently, not as infallible superheroes or perpetual villains, but as actual human beings doing their best to love and parent you. When you recognize the many different hats your parents wear, you will look at them in a new way, and that shift will open the door to a deeper, more compassionate relationship. And that's a gift for both of you.

CHAPTER 4 :
When Mom Is the Dad and Dad Is Mom or Both

The traditional idea of family roles, 'Mom' as the nurturer and 'Dad' as the provider, has evolved significantly over the years. While we can still see the norm all around us, and rightfully so, these changes are here to stay and may continue to change. Families now tend to look different from those in older TV shows or books. Perhaps your mom is the one working late hours to support the family while your dad stays home to help with homework. Or maybe your dad is a fantastic cook who ensures you're well-fed while your mom takes charge of planning your school activities and family schedules.

Those days are over when there were fixed and strict roles in a family. What really matters is not who does what but the love, hard work, and commitment both parents have to offer. Your mom may be the disciplinarian, setting the rules and making sure they're obeyed, while your dad is the soft-spoken caretaker. Or perhaps they switch off on a daily basis, depending on the day, the circumstance, or their emotional reserve. Families are fluid, and their capacity to shift in response to changing needs is an asset to be valued.

Why Do Role Reversals Happen?

Role reversals or non-traditional arrangements often happen because of practical circumstances or personal strengths. Maybe your mom has a demanding career that requires late hours or travel, so your dad steps up in ways traditionally associated with moms. Or perhaps your dad's personality makes him more patient when explaining math homework, while your mom is great at motivating you to try out for the debate team or do something crazy. To be fair, it always makes sense for both of them to do what works best for the family and it's important that you understand your role in this mix. These shifts aren't failures of tradition—they're responses to what works best for your family. This flexibility also reflects the evolving nature of modern parenting.

In some cases, I have seen families make these role shifts and transition over the span of their lives because, like it or not, sometimes either parents or both are burnt out and need a break, and maybe sometimes the break is from you! Have you ever had your parents go on a date or a vacation without you and it suddenly looks like they love each other much more than you? Its like they suddenly realize that they love themselves more? Those are the recovery bolts from having to juggle life, bills, and you.

Today's parents are more likely to share responsibilities, breaking away from gendered expectations to ensure their children's needs are met, which is such a good thing to do. By stepping into roles that might not have been expected of them, your parents show that their ultimate priority is you.

When One Parent Is Both

Sometimes, the parent is just **one** and it wouldn't be right not to acknowledge that.

Whether due to separation, divorce, or loss, there are situations where it's just **Mom** or **Dad** raising you. And that's okay. You're not left out or missing something; your experience is just different, which holds its own unique strength. In fact, you have a rare opportunity to be deeply centered on one parent instead of two. Your bond can be incredibly strong, but it also means that sometimes, **more grace is required of you** to support them, just as they support you. It can be difficult at times, especially when you feel the weight of what's missing, but this is where you must come correct. You have to be patient, understanding, and aware that they're doing their best, often carrying responsibilities meant for two. Just as they show up for you, **you have the power to show up for them too** — not by taking on their burdens, but by being the kind of child who acknowledges their efforts, appreciates their sacrifices, and gives them the love and respect they deserve.

What Can You Learn from This?

Seeing your parents adapt and switch roles can teach you valuable lessons about flexibility, teamwork, and breaking stereotypes. As an older child, you may be fortunate enough to notice that your dad is given paternity leave so he can be home to support your mom or maybe just sometimes to be home with you. It takes strength and sometimes denying themselves some gratification to do that. You might learn that strength doesn't look the same for everyone and that caregiving or providing doesn't depend on gender but on effort and love. You might also gain insight into how much work goes into raising a family and the sacrifices both parents make to ensure you have the best opportunities.

At times, these role reversals might confuse you or even cause tension. For instance, if your dad enforces rules or disciplines you in ways your mom used to, you might resist because it feels different or unexpected. Or if your mom takes charge in ways your dad used to, you might feel unsure about how to respond. There is always room to have open conversations with them. I know sometimes parents always feel the need to show a united front, but during those dinner times it's always a good topic. That way, you're able to understand your parents and know who you're dealing with. These switches are not an avenue to manipulate your parents into doing what you want, but recognizing these adjustments as efforts to keep your family running smoothly can help you appreciate the big picture and learn how you can contribute to making the family better. Don't ask me how you're going to contribute. Ask them!

Acknowledging the Unique Contributions

Every parent has their strengths, and role reversals often highlight them. Maybe your dad is the emotional anchor who helps you navigate social challenges, while your mom is the practical thinker who guides your career aspirations. Or perhaps your parents share these responsibilities equally, blurring the lines of traditional roles altogether. By focusing on the contributions they make rather than the labels assigned to them, you can see their efforts in a new light. It is wrong as kids to compare your parents or measure them against each other. Every parent gives in their own way, and just because one provides more of something—whether it's money, gifts, time, or affection—does not mean the other is worth any less.

Parents do go through difficult patches, sometimes even too difficult for the other adults to support. Sometimes, one parent needs to actually step up in the home to keep things going and sometimes it's going to be You! Yes, although society always puts a bow on what's expected and what's not. Occasionally, it comes down to you to talk sense into everyone. No matter what's happening or what role you're playing, looking down on a parent because of what's happening, what they're going through, or what you feel is unfair and hurtful.

Parents are people, too, with their own struggles, limitations, and ways of showing love. Instead of judging or choosing sides, try to understand and appreciate them both for who they are and what they bring to the table. And no, this isn't just something that 'doesn't concern you' — you're not just a kid. You have the power to bring kindness into your home, to acknowledge what each parent offers, to make sure neither one feels unappreciated, and to also remind them that you see these things and you are grateful. Do something about it. Be fair, be grateful, and remember that love is not about keeping score. There is something you're going to realize when it all boils down...they are wonderful and you will learn to love them. They are unique and wonderful in their own way.

Breaking Free from Stereotypes

For kids, it is simple to soak up what society says parents 'should' be like. However, moving beyond that helps you appreciate your family's individuality more. It does not matter whether your family fits into a template; it's about the love and support that underpin it. When you release expectations from tradition, you become open to a deeper connection with your parents as human beings.

Breaking free of the stereotype begins with realizing that each house is unique. You should be able to tell how things go in your family without fear of judgment or feeling like something is wrong simply because it doesn't fit someone else's story. It's a learning curve, one that makes you better and more empathetic who understands that life doesn't come in one shape. Differences do not imply something is broken; they simply mean that each family has its own rhythm.

There's value in embracing the confidence of your home. Maybe your dad is spending more time with you—not because he's just lucky, but because he's navigating a career transition, taking a break, or even searching for new opportunities. Maybe your mom has stepped away from work for a while, not because she 'gave up,' but because she's prioritizing something important in life. These aren't failures. They are just stages, the same that you experience growing up as a kid. Parents are human beings as well, and just as children require nurturing, so do they.

Instead of being embarrassed or comparing, children must understand these variations as teachings. There are some households with working moms, stay-at-home dads, parents with long working hours, or parents trying to make do. There isn't a 'wrong' configuration among any of them. What is essential is setting the ground in a manner where parents and children equally feel appreciated and nurtured. By shattering the stereotype, we provide an environment where all—children and parents—can develop with respect, love, and compassion. It's alright to be different!

Celebrating Your Family's Teamwork

This chapter is about teamwork. Your parents are co-parents in raising you, even though their style or function may be different. Each function they serve is a part of the puzzle that completes your family. Your parents bending, compromising, and adapting to support one another and care for you is one of the greatest displays of teamwork you will ever witness.

Life is not easy, and yet they manage to work through its difficulties just to ensure that you're all right. That's something you should look up to and learn from—not only about parenting but about life as well. After growing up, you'll know that teamwork is not merely the division of labor; it's about sacrificing for each other, doing what needs to be done, and knowing when to take charge or step aside. Their capacity to stand by one another during difficult times isn't weakness; it's wisdom.

It's what enables them to continue, even when things become too much.

And that's a lesson for you as well. Life will send obstacles your way, and sometimes you'll need a rest. That's alright. You don't have to do it all by yourself. Just like your parents work off each other, you can learn to rely on those people who love you. Request assistance, catch your breath, and realize that true strength is not about doing it all by yourself; it's about knowing when to trust and rely on others. The greatest teams aren't those where everyone does the same; they're the ones where people are there for one another when it counts most.

By knowing and valuing these dynamics, you can deepen your connection with your parents and learn to appreciate the diversity of their work. It's not, after all, about who does what—it's about how they work together to support and love you.

CHAPTER 5:

Why Parents Team Up Against You

It's one of the most annoying experiences growing up: you plead your case with one parent, hoping to get a 'yes,' but instead hear the dreaded words, "Let me speak to your mom/dad first." Then suddenly, a minute later, you are face-to-face with a joint 'no.' It feels so unjust, as if your parents are conspiring against you just to cause you trouble.

But the fact of the matter is, when your parents gang up on you, it's seldom about withholding joy or freedom from you; it's about teamwork. They're together deciding things that they think are best for you, even if those things may not be what you'd prefer. No matter what, in this case, two heads really are better than one!

Why Do Parents Join Forces?

Parents teaming up stems from their shared goal: to love, direct, and take care of you. By acting united, their objective is to offer consistent rules and expectations. If you get a "yes" from one parent and a "no" from another, it may confuse or annoy you. Joint decision-making will ensure clarity and prevent you from playing one parent against the other, even without meaning to.

Their collaboration also indicates a deeper value: respect for one another's input. When your parents discuss between themselves prior to making a decision, they're demonstrating that they respect one another's opinions and desire to be on the same page. This being on the same page provides a stable ground for your upbringing, even though it may seem like they're 'teaming up' against you presently. You ought to learn from this, it's always a good idea to seek their advice in your business.

It's Not About Ruining Your Fun

Let's be honest: hearing a 'no' for an answer can be heartbreaking, especially after putting up your case strongly to request something you desire. Nevertheless, the other side of the coin is that your parents don't intend to put an end to your enjoyment; they never do. Instead, they're looking down the road, calculating the possible consequences you may not yet be able to perceive. For instance, when they refuse to go to a late party or hang out with a group of friends, it's not that they want you to miss out. They're probably concerned about your safety, your sleep, or the type of place you'd be going into.

Their protective natures may seem restrictive, but they're done out of concern. Together, your parents are trying to make well-rounded, considered decisions in your best interest, even if those decisions aren't the ones you had your heart set on. You'd be a valuable addition to their team!

The Hidden Benefits of a United Front

When your parents work as a team, it is actually for the best, even when it doesn't seem that way at first. Here's why:

Consistency Builds Trust: The fact that your parents are of like minds serves to create stability.

You may not agree with their response, but at least you know it is a carefully thought-out choice.

Lessons Learned in Cooperation: Observing your parents cooperate with each other, even in a small manner like establishing rules, instills within you the importance of communication and cooperation.

Steering Clear of Manipulation (Even Unintentional): If parents didn't agree on decisions, it might cause confusion—or even moments when you might inadvertently take advantage of the difference between their ideas to obtain what you want.

What's Really Going On When They Say No

When parents do say "no," it does feel unfair, but ever questioned why? Sometimes, they simply wish to teach you responsibility and become more responsible. If you ask them why, you will likely see their point better!

It's also worth remembering that parents do not always see eye to eye. Behind the scenes, they may have discussed or even bickered about what the correct answer should be. The 'united front' you see is often achieved through compromise. One parent may have had to relinquish their original point in order to uphold the other's view, demonstrating to you that parenting choices do involve working together and making sacrifices.

How to Navigate These Moments

Getting frustrated or feeling defeated upon hearing a 'no' is natural. Instead of dwelling on your disappointment, try these:

Ask Them Why: Politely inquiring as to why they made their choice demonstrates maturity and may even lead to a conversation. Hearing their side doesn't necessarily mean they will change their minds, but it can make you feel heard.

Share Your Feelings: If their choice seems unfair, tell them how you feel calmly and respectfully. Phrases such as, "I know you have reasons, but I feel disappointed because..." can indicate to them that you're willing to talk things over.

Seek Out Compromises: Is there a middle ground? If they said no to a sleepover, perhaps they'd be more comfortable with you staying until

10 pm instead. Offering alternatives demonstrates that you're willing to work around their concerns.

The Bigger Picture

Your parents' teamwork may not always lead to your desired outcome, which may be upsetting, it's an indication of their dedication to raise you up correctly to the best of their capabilities. Therefore, instead of viewing it as a hindrance, try to analyze their one-front approach as a manifestation of love and concern. They care about you deeply—and sometimes, that entails a united no. As infuriating as it is, you may come to admire one day the creative effort they invest in collectively making decisions. Their capacity to hold firm together, even during challenging times, is an exercise in collaboration and respect. And even though their choices may not always seem 'fair' to you at the time, they're nearly always guided by the same purpose: supporting you in developing into a capable, content, and healthy individual.

CHAPTER 6 :
Parents Aren't Always Right

Spoiler alert: your parents aren't perfect. They are humans, and like all humans, they make mistakes, misjudge situations, and occasionally let their emotions get the better of them. Surprising? Maybe not, especially if you've ever found yourself thinking, 'They just don't get it.' The truth is, parents don't have all the answers, and sometimes, they get it wrong. Whether it's a choice they made in fear, a misinterpretation of your motives, or a response influenced by outmoded beliefs, your parents' mistakes aren't a reflection of their love for you.

Admitting this flaw, which is natural really, doesn't necessarily mean you don't love or respect them. In fact, learning how to handle these situations can actually make your relationship stronger. By realizing why parents do things wrong and learning how to approach them respectfully, you can create an opportunity for improved communication and understanding.

Why Parents Get It Wrong Sometimes

Here are some of the most common reasons why parents may not always be right:

Fear of the Unknown: Parenting involves a perpetual fear of keeping you safe and healthy. This fear can sometimes get the better of them, leading them to overreact or make overly cautious choices.

Diverse Upbringings: Your parents' conceptions of life and rules frequently have their origins in the way they were raised. If they were raised in a strict or conventional home, they may bring those principles with them into their parenting, even though they don't necessarily apply to your life anymore.

Miscommunication: Sometimes, your parents may misread your actions, words, or intentions. A joke may be taken out of context, or a simple mistake may be interpreted as a conscious decision.

Old Ideas: The world is changing fast, and concepts regarding education, relationships, and even technology are changing along with it. Your parents may still stick to ideas that were valid in their days but are no longer applicable to your reality.

Emotional Reactions: Parents are humans, too, which means they get tired, stressed, or frustrated. These emotions can affect their decisions and sometimes lead to overreactions.

Parents aren't born knowing everything. They learn as they go, just like you. Even with their best intentions, mistakes are inevitable. Parents can be wrong, and that's okay—they're human too. Sometimes, because of their own upbringing, they assume that what happened to them will happen to you, even when times have changed. They may project their fears onto you, worrying that you'll make the same mistakes they did or face the same struggles, even when your path is completely different. Sometimes, their choices may be based on personal wants instead of what's best for you—such as when a parent insists you join a team, a school, or a career path simply because it's part of their legacy. We've all witnessed it—parents insisting that you attend their alma mater or do what they did, even though it's not what you desire.

Parents are also incorrect when they push their views at you and do not allow you to respond with your own opinions. A good parent hears you out, but love can sometimes cause them to become overbearing or controlling. And let's be honest— sometimes they're wrong in a way that appears as if they're helping you, such as bending the rules excessively or covering up for you too much. You know the truth deep within, and though it is born of love, at times, it can form nasty habits.

Above all, parents can be wrong because they don't know everything. Every time you venture out into the world, you learn something new— something they might not have lived through or known about. And here's the thing: they can learn from you as well. The trick is trust-building. When you show them that you're thinking for yourself, making sound decisions, and developing into your own individual, they'll begin to realize that there's more than one way to do things. It's a process, but with time, patience, and integrity, you can lead them to understand that sometimes the student becomes the teacher.

What to Do When They're Wrong

When you find out your parents have erred, you might want to respond with anger or frustration. But responding calmly and kindly is much more productive. In order to approach the situation positively, it is advisable to pause and think for a while. Before you engage in a conversation, consider why you feel they're mistaken. Are you angry because their choice seems unjust, or do you have specific reasons why it doesn't work? Knowing your emotions will make you communicate better. Timing is crucial. Pick the right moment, and don't mention sensitive issues when your parents are under pressure or preoccupied. Catch them in a relaxed moment when they will be more receptive.

It is always a good idea to start the conversation by acknowledging their point of view. Begin with empathy; it makes the difference. For instance, "I know you're concerned about my safety, and I appreciate that…." This is a sign of respect and makes them more receptive to hearing what you have to say. Then, present your views calmly and simply. Never accuse them of being in error; rather, work on why you perceive things differently. Say things like, "I see what you mean, but this is why I feel this way."

Ask questions because sometimes their logic isn't as apparent to you as it is to them. If you ask questions such as, "Can you explain why you did that?" this can help both parties better understand one another. I never visit my mom without having a different plan in mind. If their decision feels unfair, offer a compromise. Showing that you're willing to meet halfway demonstrates maturity and respect.

This I have discovered to be highly effective even with other individuals beyond my family such as my challenging bosses!

What Happens Next?

Even when you respond flawlessly, your parents may not apologize right away for being wrong. That's fine. Sometimes, they need time to think and realize your point of view. Sometimes, they may insist that their choice was correct, even though you can't see it that way. Remember that parents, like everyone else, have egos. Admitting one's errors is not easy, particularly when they feel a great sense of responsibility to care for and direct you. If they cannot accept that they made a mistake, do not take offense. I truly appreciate that today's parents are also realizing it is okay to say sorry and that by reading a book such as this, for instance, young people like you can see that them being expressive does not mean that they are weak.

When your parents do finally say they were wrong, which does not happen very often, it can be a big deal. Accept their apology and thank them for being honest. This is a turning point in your relationship, demonstrating that both of you are willing to learn and grow together.

When You Disagree, But They Won't Budge

There will be occasions when you still think your parents are in the wrong, but they won't budge. At such times, it's necessary to choose your battles. Ask yourself:

- Is it a life-altering choice, or can I live with it?

- Can I work around this in some way without creating conflict?

- Is this a time when patience and comprehension could do more good than quarreling?

At other times, the best thing to do is to drop it and come back to it later when emotions have settled.

What You Learn from Their Mistakes

Ironically, your parents' errors can be a valuable learning experience. Yeah, digest it as strange as it may sound. When they mess up, they're teaching you the way of imperfection. Observe how they bounce back—whether they own up, learn, or grow from the lesson—so that you, too, can handle your own errors with poise. Errors also remind you that nobody has all the answers. This understanding can promote compassion, and you can start viewing your parents as individuals who are doing their best in a tough job.

When parents mess up, it's not the end of the world—it's a chance to learn. For them, it's a chance to rethink their strategy. For you, it's a chance to exercise patience, empathy, and good communication. Working through these moments with kindness and respect doesn't only resolve the problem at hand; it builds the foundation of your relationship. By embracing their humanity and handling disagreements constructively, you'll build a deeper connection that goes beyond authority and rules—a connection rooted in mutual understanding and love.

CHAPTER 7:
When You Know Better

Sometimes, there is no denying the fact that you just know better. Be it new technology, a school policy, or even a better way to handle a tricky situation, there are moments when your knowledge outpaces your parents'. There is nothing degrading in it, nor does it make them unintelligent or unwilling to learn. It has more to do with the rapidly evolving world. As a person growing up in it, you are at the forefront of the changes taking place and can relate to them more than your parents.

However, it poses a dilemma: knowing something your parents don't, can feel tricky. They are supposed to be the ones with more knowledge, aren't they? The tricky part is how to share your insight without making them feel embarrassed, outdated, or challenged. Striking the balance between offering suggestions and respecting their authority requires tact, empathy, and understanding their perspective.

Why This Happens

Your parents grew up in a different time, with different norms, technologies, and ideas about how the world works. Talk about a generational gap! While they've gained wisdom through experience, they might not have kept up with every new development. It is humanly impossible. On the other end of the spectrum, you are immersed in the latest trends, ideas, and technologies, whether through school, friends, or the internet.

For example, you might understand the intricacies of a smartphone app or game better than they do. You've probably been taught more up-to-date information about science, social issues, or technology in school. Similarly, nowadays, there is more talk about mental well-being, which didn't exist a couple of decades ago. These cultural shifts weren't as prominent when they were growing up. Hence, the piece of information that came to you naturally was alien to them.

This isn't a competition of who knows more; it's a natural result of living in different eras. But when these knowledge gaps come into play, it can create tension if not handled well.

Why Parents May Struggle to Accept This

Understanding why your parents might react defensively or dismissively when you know something they don't is important. They often see themselves as your guide and protector. They might feel like their role is being questioned when you know more about something. Your approach to communicating what you know really counts, and you must wield it carefully. New information, especially if it contradicts what they've always believed, can be intimidating and breeds a lot of fear. It forces them to confront the idea that their knowledge might not be as relevant anymore. I know a lot of people who hate change and are afraid of it, though change is a real thing — the only constant of this ever-changing world.

If you present your knowledge in a way that feels like a challenge, they might perceive it as undermining their authority, even if that's not your intention. Understanding these emotional responses can help you approach the situation with more sensitivity.

How to Share What You Know Without Conflict

Be Patient. Your parents may not understand immediately or accept what you're saying, especially at the beginning, but don't get frustrated. Remember, change takes time. They might require space and time to process the new reality and ideas.

Frame It as a Collaboration. Rather than saying, "You're wrong' or "I know better," use things like, "May I demonstrate to you a different approach?" or "Here's something I just learned about, what do you think?" I don't know if I am meant to put this here, but I had this trick where I would always take something I learned from my mom and use it as an anchor to present my ideas.

Share Respectfully. Respect their experience and wisdom, even as you share your own insights. For instance, "I know you've been dealing with this for a long time, but I came across something new that could be helpful." Don't bring up your knowledge in the midst of an argument or when they're most upset. Instead, wait until they're calm and more likely to be receptive.

Use Evidence, Not Ego. Back up your knowledge with facts or examples. If you're explaining something like a new technology, show them how it works rather than just telling them they're wrong.

No matter how hard you try, there will be occasions when your parents push back against your knowledge. They may dismiss it outright, debate against it, or dig in deeper with their own views. When this occurs, it's important to remain calm and not turn the situation into a battle of wills. Ask yourself: Is this a matter of life and death, or can I let it go? Can I lead by example rather than trying to be right? Would they be more receptive to this suggestion if I mentioned it a little later or went about it another way?

Sometimes, your actions will speak louder than your words. If you're trying to show them a better way to approach a problem, demonstrating it through your own behavior can be more effective than explaining it.

Why Your Perspective Matters

It's simple to feel as though your parents have all the control in the relationship, but your input is more important than you realize. By sharing your information in a considerate and respectful manner, you assist in creating a dynamic in which both parties are able to learn and develop. Your opinion allows your parents to experience life from your perspective. It keeps them in touch with new ideas, trends, and thinking they may not otherwise be exposed to. They may even come to depend on you as a go-to source of information and insight over time.

Although you may know more about some things, your parents have lots of life experience to share. They've made mistakes, been through challenges, and learned from them that you haven't experienced yet. You can approach issues together by combining your fresh perspective with their experience in a manner neither of you could have done. They may provide emotional understanding or straightforward advice that complements your technical acumen. As a first-generation college graduate, many of the things my mother imposed were an attempt to help me do far better than she did. Their life experiences can help you put a situation into perspective and their advice can serve as a moral or ethical filter for effective usage of your knowledge.

Building a Collaborative Relationship

Approaching such dicey situations as opportunities for collaboration rather than conflict helps you create a relationship where both sides feel valued and respected. Here's what that might look like:

- For You: you feel empowered to share your knowledge without fear of rejection or criticism.

- For Them: they feel respected and appreciated, even when you know something they don't.

- For Your Relationship: you build a foundation of mutual trust and understanding that strengthens your bond over time.

Even when you're certain you're correct, at times it's best not to argue much. Perhaps your parents aren't quite ready to accept something new, or perhaps the problem isn't worth the conflict that might result. Picking your battles is a sign of maturity and serves to maintain your relationship. When you know more, it isn't about showing your parents how wrong they are or proving yourself better. It's about teaching them in a way that allows both of you to grow. Bringing in another supportive adult to assist you in putting forward your point can also be a consideration. By entering these moments in a humble, empathetic, and cooperative state of mind, you can prompt your parents to learn from you as you've learned from them. In the process, you'll create a relationship that thrives on mutual respect, open communication, and a shared commitment to learning and growing together. And that's a win for everyone.

CHAPTER 8 :
Be Kind to Them Anyway

There are days when your parents will feel like the biggest obstacle in your life. They'll say "no" when you were hoping for a "yes," ask questions when you just want to be left alone, or give advice that feels out of touch with your world. On those days, frustration builds, patience wears thin, and kindness feels like the last thing you want to offer.

But here's the thing: kindness is one of the most powerful tools you have. By choosing to be kind, even in difficult moments, you are opening the door to understanding, growth, and a stronger relationship with your parents. It is my most "lethal" tool to disarm my mom! Have you ever had an issue with your mom and seen the way she tries to get back on your good side by making your favorite food for dinner? You can do that too!

Why Kindness Matters

Kindness is more than just being polite or avoiding conflict. It's a way of saying, "I see you. I value you. I care about our relationship." And that's something your parents need to hear, just like you do. Your parents are human, and like all humans, they have good days and bad days. Sometimes, they may be reacting from an overload of other things spilling into the home. They might carry stress from work, worry about bills, or feel unsure how to connect with you. When you offer kindness, you allow them to let their guard down and meet you with the same energy. However, kindness doesn't mean agreeing with everything they say or ignoring your own feelings. It's about choosing to respond with compassion, even when you're upset or hurt.

Having said that, being kind isn't always easy. There are moments when frustration takes over, you feel like they don't deserve your kindness, or you're just too tired to try. But that's when kindness matters most. Why? Because kindness isn't about earning points or being right; it's about creating a connection. It's about showing up as the best version of yourself, even when it's hard.

Practice kindness when it feels impossible by:

- Taking a Breath: when emotions run high, pause for a moment. Take a deep breath and remind yourself that responding with anger or frustration won't help.

- Empathizing: try to put yourself in their shoes. What might they be feeling? What pressures or fears could be influencing their actions?

- Choosing Your Words Wisely: instead of snapping or yelling, take a moment to think about what you want to say and how you can say it respectfully.

- Focusing on the Bigger Picture: ask yourself, "Will this matter a week from now? A month? A year?" Often, the things that upset us aren't as important as they feel.

Small acts of kindness go a long way, and they don't have to be grand or dramatic. Often, small things make the biggest difference. A thank you, even if it's for something small, like making dinner or giving you a ride, shows that you notice and appreciate their efforts—express your gratitude. A dashing smile can lighten the mood and remind them that you care. Compliment them! I cannot tell you how much I love hearing my colleagues, who have kids, talk about what their kids said about what they wore to the office. Helping out without being asked, whether it's doing the dishes, tidying up, or running an errand, shows that you're willing to pitch in.

Kindness is also letting your parents talk and really hearing what they have to say, even if you don't agree.

What Kindness Looks Like in Conflict

Kindness takes so many forms. Conflict is inevitable in any relationship, and your relationship with your parents is no exception. But even in the middle of an argument, kindness can change the tone and outcome.

Stay Calm: it's okay to feel upset, but try not to let anger take over. Speak calmly and avoid yelling or blaming.

Use "I" Statements: instead of saying, "You never listen to me," try, "I feel unheard when you interrupt me." This shifts the focus from blame to your feelings.

Acknowledge Their Perspective: even if you disagree, let them know you understand where they're coming from. "I get that you're worried about me, but I want to share how I see it."

Apologize When Necessary: if you've said or done something hurtful, own up to it. A sincere apology can go a long way in healing hurt feelings.

When you choose kindness, you're not just improving your relationship with your parents but setting an example for how relationships should work. You're showing them that even in moments of disagreement or frustration, respect and compassion can prevail. Kindness often creates a ripple effect. When you approach your parents with understanding, they're more likely to respond in kind. Over time, this can transform the way you communicate and solve problems together.

Kindness isn't just something you give to others; it's something you owe to yourself, too. If you're feeling overwhelmed, misunderstood, or unheard, it's important to acknowledge those feelings and give yourself the space to process them. Practice self-kindness by taking breaks. If a conversation with your parents becomes too intense, step away and take a breather. Imagine saying, "Dad, let's just calm down and take a breather, I am sure we can talk about this when we're calmer." It would be phenomenal!

Find an outlet to express yourself. Write in a journal, talk to a friend, or find another healthy way to process your emotions. I play 3 instruments and ran track, and let me tell you, they did wonders for me.

Lastly, make sure you celebrate your efforts. Recognize the times when you choose kindness, even when it was hard. That takes strength and maturity.

Kindness as a Superpower

In a divided, competitive, and combative world, kindness is a superpower. It's a choice to create bridges rather than walls, find understanding rather than battle, and love rather than be right. When you decide to be kind to your parents, even on hard days, you're not only building the relationship, you're becoming the person who can navigate life with grace, compassion, and strength.

So the next time your parents get on your nerves, take a deep breath and recall: kindness can turn even the toughest moments. Treat them kindly anyway. It's worth it.

CHAPTER 9:
Other Parents

When experiencing and navigating life's challenges, your parents are often your first stop for advice and support. But they aren't your only source of wisdom. The world is full of alternative resources and perspectives that can complement their guidance and help you grow in ways you might not have imagined.

Building a Network of Trusted Advisors

Your parents may know a lot, but they don't know everything—and that's okay. As a kid, I used to be so envious of my brother because he had very present godparents. I'm sure this happens in many cultures and regions: there are always key people who step in and play a role in raising you, even if they aren't your parents. They've probably been around for as long as you can remember, maybe even longer. They support you, cheer you on, and offer guidance in ways you don't always realize until later. Some of them are your mom's friends, bosses, or colleagues—people she loves, respects, and spends time with. Others might be family members, like grandparents, who shape your life in ways you never expected.

For me, a lot of what I learned about entrepreneurship and running a business came from my grandmother. She was phenomenal. Despite not having a formal education, she had an incredible work ethic, sharp instincts, and a way of handling things that left a lasting impact on me. She didn't require a degree to educate me on resilience, resourcefulness, and hard work.

And if you don't have any of those figures in your life, that's alright too. Family isn't blood—it's the people who show up, care, and invest in you. Sometimes, those people find you along the way. The most important thing is knowing that support can be different, and it counts no matter where it is. Teachers, coaches, mentors, and other adults are some of the other sources in your life who can give you insight that your parents may not be experienced or knowledgeable enough to give. For example, a teacher could assist you in overcoming academic struggles or investigating career interests. A mentor in a sport or hobby could encourage you to learn new skills or overcome adversity. Even older siblings and friends can be sources of advice, providing insights that are more familiar to your own lives.

The secret is developing a varied network of individuals you can reach out to for assistance. Everyone has their own set of experiences and knowledge, so your network becomes a valuable asset to help you navigate life's ups and downs.

Learning from Books, Podcasts, and Other Media

The world is full of individuals and resources that can guide you through the complexities of life. These people can offer insights that your parents may not be able to. Each of them has their own experience, view, and skill set, and they can help complete the missing pieces when you require guidance that you cannot get from your parents.

Unlike personal advice, media resources are often created by experts who've spent years studying or experiencing the topics they discuss.

They offer the benefit of specialized knowledge, presented in ways that are accessible and engaging. Learning from online sources is a great way to expand your knowledge, but it comes with a huge responsibility: **trust, but verify**. You can't believe everything you see online. I have noticed people diagnosing themselves with all sorts of ailments on Instagram and TikTok. Quite honestly, some of it is so over-the-top and misleading that it's both cringeworthy and laughable. Just because something is convincing to you doesn't mean it is true. We need to be cautious about what we listen to and accept online because misinformation travels very quickly, and not everything is supported by actual knowledge or experience.

If you haven't yet got a phone, you're likely to reach that stage where you do and when there are fewer limits on what you can see. But even when you are an adult, you need to keep protecting your mind, ensuring what you expose yourself to is truly helpful, accurate, and not simply random views masquerading as facts. Media materials can be a wonderful source of advice, just like this excellent book you're reading, but then again, there are hundreds of sources out there that aren't. The key is to question, fact-check, and think critically about everything you're taking in. Don't accept information at face value—challenge it, investigate it, and ensure that it really does hold up. As you search through these resources, don't forget to remain critical, ask actual people in your life.

I used to have a proverb that read, "In the multitude of counselors there is safety." Be unapologetic about seeking a fifth opinion on something. Not all advice works, and some sources may not appeal to your values or needs. Seek out reputable authors, experts, or creators who share points of view that work for you, just like I do!

The Role of Professional Guidance

In life, you will face issues that need the assistance of experts. Counselors, therapists, or coaches can offer tools and strategies tailored to your specific situation. For instance, if you have issues with mental health, a school counselor or therapist can assist you in understanding your feelings and how to deal with them in a healthy manner. If you are searching for a career, a guidance counselor or career coach can assist you in identifying your strengths and possibilities. It takes strength to seek professional assistance. It is a sign of your willingness to care for yourself and improve.

Seeking Wisdom from Peers and Friends

Although adults may be more seasoned, your friends can also provide excellent advice. Friends who have struggled with issues of their own or comprehend the subtleties of where you are in life are excellent sounding boards. Discussing a problem with a friend may provide you with insight, and shared experience makes their recommendations even more valid. Again, be aware that, as with any source of advice, peer advice is not perfect. It's always a good idea to balance their advice with your own intuition and values. Occasionally, the best advice is gained by venturing out of your comfort zone and experiencing other cultures, traditions, and thought processes. Reading books, watching documentaries, and talking to others who have had varying experiences can broaden your mind to alternative ideas and methods.

This wider understanding can make you perceive your issues differently and even enable you to understand your parents better. For example, discovering your parents' upbringing or their cultural background might help you justify their actions. Likewise, gaining insights into different modes of thought can provide you with new solutions to tackle your own problems.

But you must always check out the information you receive to make your best decisions. It is alright to decline advice, too, so don't ever feel obligated to accept it. It's also alright to sleep on it. I have always found sleeping on things to be extremely rewarding.

Evaluating the Quality of Advice

Not all advice is the same; some is super helpful, some might not make sense right away, and some might not be right at all. Whether advice comes from your parents, a mentor, or an online article, it's important to think critically and see what truly fits your situation. Ask yourself, is this advice based on facts or opinions? Does it align with my values and goals? Has it worked for others in similar situations?

Learning to think critically about advice will help you filter out noise and focus on what's truly useful. This skill will serve you well throughout life, enabling you to make informed decisions that reflect your unique circumstances. Again, just like media resources, verify every information you get. It would do you more harm than good, no matter who is saying it. Search within your heart and decide. Feel free to loop multiple sources together, I have seen that two adults are less likely to misguide you. There is something about saying, "I am going to run this with my mom and dad as well to see what they think," and doing it!

Your Parents Aren't Being Replaced

Being open to "outside" guidance and advice doesn't mean you're ignoring or disrespecting your parents. Instead, it's a sign of maturity and independence. It shows you're thinking about your growth as an individual and seeking out the best tools and perspectives available.

An important thing to note here is that it is possible that you may not find a solution that perfectly fits your situation. Thus, you have to create your own best-fit formula by combining your parents' wisdom with other sources of guidance. The insights you gain elsewhere can even help you improve communication with your parents, giving you new ways to understand and connect with them.

Becoming a Source of Guidance Yourself

As you mature and gain experience, you'll begin to form your own opinion. You may find yourself becoming a guide for your younger siblings, classmates, or even your parents. This transition is a natural evolution of growing up. It does not indicate that you've surpassed your parents, but that you're emerging as an equal partner in solving life's problems. Giving back by sharing what you've learned with others is a means of building your relationships.

When you become a source of wisdom for others—a friend, a younger brother or sister, or even someone older who admires you—there's an unstated **code of honor** that comes with it: **be honest and never be deceitful**. Offering advice, sharing information, or assisting someone through a situation is a privilege, not an opportunity to sound smart or powerful. Misinformation, even accidental, can have real-world consequences. If you don't know something, it's better to admit it than make something up. If you're not sure, ask them to double-check or get a second opinion. Honesty builds trust, and once folks view you as a trustworthy source, your words mean something—so choose them carefully. Being honest doesn't require you to be cruel or condescending; it requires leading with integrity, acknowledging when you're wrong, and always seeking to be someone others can rely on for actual support, not convenient or inflated tales.

The Beauty of Shared Wisdom

Life is filled with questions and challenges, and no one has all the answers—not even your parents. It's not their fault, as humans, we can't have the knowledge of everything. Therefore, it is inevitable to seek guidance from various sources.

You are equipping yourself with the tools required to make thoughtful, informed decisions.

Remember, wisdom is everywhere; you just need to identify it. It can be a heartfelt conversation with a mentor, a lesson from a trusted friend, or a chapter in a book; every piece of guidance contributes to your growth, so don't take anything lightly. There will come a stage in your life where you'll realize that the best guidance isn't about solving problems; it's about building connections, understanding yourself, and becoming a source of light for others.

CHAPTER 10 :
The Unspoken Lessons

Not everything your parents teach comes with a lecture or a set of instructions. Some of the most important lessons are taught without words—through actions, habits, and how they navigate the world. These unspoken lessons shape your understanding of life, often more profoundly than the verbal advice they give. After all, it is often said that children imitate their parents' actions, not their words.

Actions Speak Louder Than Words

"Do as I say, not as I do" is something you may have heard, but action speaks louder than words could ever possibly do. Your parents' decisions, actions, and habits teach you about their values and priorities.

For example, check how they treat others. If your parents are respectful to strangers, help without expecting anything in return, or treat friends and relatives with respect, they're teaching you compassion and generosity without saying so. If they persevere, remain steadfast in their duties, or recover from failures, they're teaching you the value of resilience and determination. Observe these small things. How they smile at the cashier, apologize when wrong, or root for you when you play says a lot about their personalities and value system.

The Way They Show Love

Love isn't always expressed in grand gestures. It can be found in the little things, the day-to-day acts like cooking your favorite food, sleeping late to assist you in a project, or putting in extra time to purchase something you require. Your parents' love language may not be what you imagine. Perhaps they don't say a lot of "I love you," but they're always there for you. Maybe their way of showing their concern is by offering advice, even when it sounds nagging. Paying attention to these subtle demonstrations of love can assist you in appreciating their efforts, even if they don't fit your ideal image of love.

Sometimes the greatest lessons aren't learned by what your parents do, but by what they let you do. When they allow you to learn from your own mistakes or back away for you to sort things out on your own, they're instilling self-reliance and independence in you. The silent endorsement—to stand aside and let you muddle through—is proof that they believe in you and your capability to learn and develop. It's a lesson in empowerment, though it doesn't necessarily feel like it at the moment.

Not every action or habit your parents model will resonate with you, and that's okay. What's important is recognizing the intention behind their actions. Perhaps they're strict on your curfew because they're concerned about your safety. Perhaps they're tightfisted because they want to save for your future. If you can see their motives, you might be able to appreciate their efforts even if you don't always agree with their actions.

Lessons That Last a Lifetime

As you grow, you'll find others—brothers and sisters, friends, or even your future children—

looking up to you for direction. The implicit teachings you've picked up from your parents can then form the foundation of how you want to inspire and lead others. By heeding these silent teachings, you're not merely learning yourself; you're readying yourself to pass on your own unspoken lessons one day.

The implicit lessons your parents teach are akin to seeds planted softly in your heart and mind. They will not be seen immediately, but will develop into the values, habits, and beliefs that shape your life. Take the time to observe them. Think about how your parents' behaviors have influenced you, and how you can take those lessons along with you. Even when they are not speaking, your parents are educating you about something worth learning, which may be the lessons that stick with you the longest.

CHAPTER 11 :
Growing Together

As you grow, your parents grow too. They're not the same individuals they were when you were born, any more than you are the same person you were as a toddler. Growth is not a one-way street; it's a mutual experience. You and your parents are learning, adapting, and changing constantly. You have to accept that shared growth and seek out new ways to bond with your parents while working through the changes of life. Relationships are not static; they're evolving and evolving.

Changing Roles

The parent-child relationship changes as you get older. When you were younger, your parents were the ultimate authority figures and decision-makers who took care of you. As you get older, the dynamics change. You become more independent, able to make decisions for yourself, and your parents begin to step back and let you take charge.

This transition may be difficult. For parents, it is hard to relinquish their protective role. For children, it may be tough to adapt to the responsibility that comes with self-reliance. Identifying this change as a normal phase of growing up can make it easier to accept and allow for mutual respect.

Open Communication

As you grow, your relationship with your parents benefits from more open and honest communication. Being able to share your thoughts, feelings, and aspirations with them can make them understand the kind of person you are aspiring to be. Similarly, showing concern for their views and experiences can strengthen your bond. Ask them how they developed over the years—what they have learned, what they have become, and what matters most to them. These conversations can bridge generational gaps and foster mutual understanding.

Learning from Each Other

Development is not only about children learning from their parents. As you learn and experience things, you get to impart knowledge to your parents, as well. Perhaps you expose them to the latest technology, give them information about a new subject they don't know much about, or open their eyes to the world from a different point of view. This sharing of thought is a two-way street. When you learn from one another, you establish an association based on cooperation and understanding.

Embracing Change Together

Change is unavoidable. You may leave home, establish a career, or have a family of your own. Your parents may retire, develop new hobbies or encounter issues of aging. Such changes can be exhilarating and overwhelming, yet they also present chances for growth and bonding. Celebrate each other's milestones and support one another during transitions. Whether a small act or a grand gesture of support, standing in for each other solidifies the bond you have.

Building an Adult Relationship

Once you enter adulthood, your relationship with your parents transforms. They can begin to view you as an equal, and you can start viewing them not merely as parents but as individuals, each with their own history, aspirations, and challenges. Building an adult relationship with them means finding a balance between maintaining the respect you've always had for them and forging a partnership based on shared experiences and understanding.

Forgiveness and Acceptance

No relationship is perfect. There will be moments of disagreement, frustration, or even hurt. Growing together means recognizing these moments as opportunities to practice forgiveness and acceptance. Your parents won't always get it right, and neither will you. But choosing to move past mistakes and focus on the love you share can strengthen your bond and help you grow closer over time.

Cherishing the Journey

As you and your parents mature, it's vital to cherish the journey you've shared and continue to share. Look back on the memories—the laughter, the lessons, and the obstacles you've overcome together. Valuing the present and anticipating the future can enable you to develop a relationship that continues to grow and flourish.

A Journey of Mutual Growth

Growing together is more than role reversal or adjusting to new situations; it's about strengthening your bond and creating a relationship based on love and respect. As you grow, be sure to notice and acknowledge your parents' growth as well. They've been with you, working through their own struggles and triumphs while helping you navigate yours.

Your relationship with your parents is a living thing, full of promise for future discovery, new understanding, and mutual growth. Take the trip, and you'll discover the bond between you grows stronger over time.